The Queen Mother

The Hulton Getty Picture Collection

The Queen Mother

The Hulton Getty Picture Collection

Roger Hudson

CASSELL&CO

First published in 2000 by Cassell & Co
Wellington House
125 Strand
London WC2R 0BB

This book was produced by The Hulton Getty Picture Collection Limited,
Unique House, 21–31 Woodfield Road, London W9 2BA

For Cassell: For Hulton Getty:
Editors: Stephen Guise, Eluned Jones Design: Tea McAleer and Alex Linghorn
Proof reader & indexer: Liz Ihre
Picture research: Sophie Spencer-Wood
Special thanks: Richard Collins

A CIP catalogue record for this book is available from the British Library.

ISBN 0304358290

Page 2: Attending one of her many engagements during the late 1960s, the Queen Mother displays her fondness for hats, strings of pearls, and the smile that has warmed so many occasions over the years.

Printed in Italy by Printer Trento Srl

Contents

Introduction

Queen Elizabeth's one hundredth birthday fell on Friday 4 August 2000 and was accompanied by a season of celebration. I was one of the congregation in St Paul's Cathedral on 11 July at the glorious service to commemorate those one hundred years. Four generations of the Royal Family were present; there were foreign kings and queens, military bands and state trumpeters playing a fanfare from the Whispering Gallery.

And of course there was the Queen Mother herself. I will never forget her slow but effortless walk down the entire length of the Cathedral or how she glanced about her, greeting those she knew. Radiant, bright of eye, and in a new soft-peach outfit, she scored another triumph.

In June she attended Garter Ceremony at Windsor on a day of broiling heat. As she stepped out of her car, there was an outburst of clapping and cheering from the crowds. I don't know how you define genuine warmth in a clap and a cheer but I do know that it was intensely moving. In the same week, she was present at four days of Royal Ascot, and at her ball, retiring that evening at 1.15 a.m.

It is popular to think of her as Britain's favourite granny – or now 'great-granny' – but the love was earned during the dark days of the Second World War. Throughout the war, she and the King were conspicuously still in London, a sign that the country was fighting on. Queen Elizabeth never wore uniform. In her well-styled coats and hats, she could be seen walking round Buckingham Palace after the bombing or visiting bomb-sites in the East End, Coventry and elsewhere. This book contains photos of the Queen with her daughters, driving a horse and cart at Sandringham, her daughters cycling beside her.

That she was a civilian somehow represented a better world worth fighting for and was a considerable contrast to the more sinister images emerging from Nazi Germany. Not for nothing did Hitler describe her as 'the most dangerous woman in Europe!'

In her own hand she wrote a long letter to President Roosevelt, and in 1942 she invited Mrs Roosevelt to come to England to see what the British were going through, an important step towards the Americans giving the vital help needed to win the war.

Her life encompasses the twentieth century and all its changes. Her family, the Strathmores were not rich. When she was young, she would come home from a dance by carriage, and had to ask why the carriage kept stopping. The coachman told her that the tired old horse was taking a nap. Latterly the helicopter has been her means of transport and she has been able to drop in all over Britain to fulfil her engagements.

Many of her sayings have been widely quoted. One is less well known. She was in hospital following an operation, and was shown the bulletin that was about to be released to the effect that Her Majesty was 'comfortable'. She told the surgeon: 'Of course comfortable means different things to the surgeon and to the patient!'

At the time of her eightieth birthday, the nation thanked her for a lifetime of service, hardly daring to expect that she would continue to serve for a further twenty years. All her life the Queen Mother has fulfilled her philosophy – that when you come into her orbit, your life must get better.

It is good to hear that she is training horses for two or three seasons ahead.

Hugo Vickers

1. A Scottish Upbringing

1900–1923

On 4 August 1900 Elizabeth Bowes-Lyon is born to Claude George Bowes-Lyon, Lord Glamis, and Nina Cecilia Cavendish-Bentick of the Duke of Portland's family. The exact place of her birth is unclear, although it is likely to have been at her family's London home in Grosvenor Gardens. Her childhood is divided between the family seat in Scotland, Glamis Castle in Angus, near Dundee, and a Queen Anne house, St Paul's Walden Bury, near Hitchin in Hertfordshire. Elizabeth is largely educated at home by foreign governesses and soon learns to speak French and German. During the First World War Glamis Castle becomes a convalescent home for wounded soldiers, with whom Lady Elizabeth becomes a great favourite, a clear indication of the humour and sociable nature that are to make her so popular in later life. She first meets Prince Albert, second son of King George V, known affectionately as 'Bertie' to his family, when she is four but does not cross his path again until 1920, when they meet at a dance. In 1921 he proposes but is turned down. However, his mother Queen Mary comes over to Glamis to inspect Lady Elizabeth and clearly approves. In January 1923, at the third time of asking, Lady Elizabeth agrees to marry the Prince, who sends a prearranged telegram to his parents: 'All Right, Bertie.'

Lady Elizabeth Angela Marguerite Bowes-Lyon, aged six or seven, nicknamed 'Princess' by her family. She wears an adaptation of the old English farm labourer's smock made popular by the illustrations of Kate Greenaway and the Arts-and-Crafts Movement at the end of the 19th century. Round her neck are strings of seed pearls, full-size versions of which she will seldom be seen without later in life.

(*Opposite*) Elizabeth, aged two, sits in her high chair. (*Right*) Aged four in 1904, the year her father inherited the title of Earl of Strathmore and Kinghorne.

Lord and Lady Strathmore with their family in about 1903. Their eldest daughter was already dead of diphtheria; Alec, seated in front, died of a brain tumour, brought on by a blow from a cricket ball, in 1911. Elizabeth's brother David, the youngest of the Strathmores' children, is on his mother's lap and Elizabeth is beside him, with ribbons in her hair.

On her pony, riding side-saddle, in front of Glamis Castle. Her favourite pony was called Bobs, but he was much darker than the one here. Elizabeth and David were known to pour water on guests from the battlements in the background.

Elizabeth and David – 'The Two Benjamins' – in about 1905. They were so called because of the gap between them and their siblings, in reference to Jacob's son Benjamin in the Old Testament.

Elizabeth and David in the Italian Garden at Glamis, which was created by their mother. The Queen Mother has always been a passionate gardener.

Paddling on the moors near to Glamis. Sunstroke was taken very seriously by the Edwardians, so floppy hats were *de rigueur*.

(*Left*) The Queen Mother's enthusiasm for hats obviously began young, no doubt inherited from her mother, who was famous throughout Scotland for her own. She poses with a spaniel, which stands no chance of competing for attention with the stunning creation on her head. (*Opposite*) Elizabeth at the Strathmores' country house in Hertfordshire, St Paul's Walden Bury, near Hitchin, where in fact the family spent more time than at Glamis.

Standing on an 18th-century chair to oblige a photographer, near one of Glamis Castle's double-barred windows.

Wearing a yet more elaborate sun hat, Elizabeth plays with a kitten at Glamis.

Mr Neall, the children's dancing master, would dance with them while playing his violin when they were called upon to entertain their parents' guests at Glamis.

Lady Strathmore, both artistic and musical, could not resist dressing up her youngest children in period costume. Elizabeth's outfit, which makes her look like some Spanish Infanta, was indeed based on a picture by Velasquez. It was cherry-pink with gold braid and buttons. The Strathmores are purportedly the last family in Scotland to have employed a jester, so David's cap-and-bells are highly suitable.

Elizabeth has taken off her hairband for this picture taken in 1912. Her brother Michael, on the right, served in the Royal Scots during the war and was wrongly reported dead when in fact he had been wounded and captured.

Looking after a
produce stall at
a wartime Red
Cross bazaar.

Glamis Castle was a convalescence home for soldiers during the First World War. Elizabeth, seen here in nursing uniform, took on duties beyond her years, especially when her mother was devastated by the death in action of her son Fergus at the Battle of Loos in 1915. Fergus served in the Black Watch along with three of his brothers, all of whom were wounded.

Sitting between her young brother David and a convalescing officer at Glamis during the war. Her sparkling personality had a tonic effect on the soldiers. 'May you be hung, drawn and quartered. Yes, hung in diamonds, drawn in a coach-and-four and quartered in the best house in the land,' wrote one in her autograph book.

At the wheel of a car in 1917, long before the days of driving tests. The motor car was just one among many symbols and means of emancipation for young women of her generation.

Poise and beauty
begin to overtake
the teenager, in
1918, though only
5ft 2ins tall.

Elizabeth 'came out', as the phrase was, in 1919, being presented at Court and attending debutante dances. This photograph, in which the famous pearls are in evidence, dates from about that time.

With her father in 1921. He wears the uniform of an honorary colonel in the Black Watch.

The first time Elizabeth achieves celebrity status is as a bridesmaid to Princess Mary, the Princess Royal, daughter of King George V and sister of her future husband, in 1922, when she married Henry, Viscount Lascelles. This was the first royal wedding to receive 20th-century-style media attention.

Her engagement to the King's second son, the Duke of York, has been announced and Elizabeth walks with her mother outside Glamis Castle for one of a number of photographs taken for the press.

Elizabeth visits an Edinburgh factory with her future husband (who wears a bowler hat) shortly before her wedding day. It is McVities' Bakery and they order their four-tier wedding cake while there. Note the cine-camera above the heads of the factory girls on the left.

A snapshot from
a family album,
taken at Glamis
Castle before
the engagement.
Bertie enjoyed
the informality of
the house parties
held there.

The Duke of York with his bride-to-be after a game of polo in 1923.

A carefully framed study taken at Glamis in 1922, by which time the Duke of York is well and truly smitten by Elizabeth's charms.

A tennis party held in London in 1923, where Elizabeth has been watching her fiancé play a game at which he excels.

2. Royal Bride and Mother
1923–1936

The marriage of the Duke and Duchess of York is the first royal wedding to take place in Westminster Abbey since the future King Richard II was married there 540 years earlier. However, it is not allowed to be broadcast on radio 'because people might hear it while sitting in public houses with their hats on'. A round of visiting schools, hospitals, factories and agricultural shows, of planting trees, of laying foundation stones, and of foreign tours soon allows the new Duchess to exercise her charm. She introduces some much needed informality into the Royal routine, shows off her social skills and disarms the gruff King George V. A stickler for punctuality, it is he who makes excuses when she is late. 'Unlike his own sons, I was never afraid of him,' she is to say much later. Princess Elizabeth is born in 1926, and after the birth of Princess Margaret in 1930 the Yorks are given Royal Lodge in Windsor Great Park as a country home. Their London house is 145 Piccadilly near Hyde Park Corner, which is bombed during the war. Royal Lodge becomes a haven of family domesticity in contrast to the somewhat louche lifestyle of the Prince of Wales at Fort Belvedere in the Park nearby. A few weeks before his death in January 1936, King George V confides to a friend, 'I pray to God that my eldest son will never marry and that nothing will come between Bertie and Lilibet and the Throne.'

Elizabeth, Duchess of York, captured in a formal pose by the photographer Bertram Park in 1926, the year she gave birth to Princess Elizabeth. Although Park found the strict rules set down by the royal family 'irksome and outdated', the photograph seems to capture perfectly the essence of the future Queen Consort.

The newly-wed couple with the bridesmaids.
The Duchess of York has laid her bouquet
on the Tomb of the Unknown Warrior in the
Abbey. Her not very becoming veil of Flanders
lace has been lent by Queen Mary. The Duke
wears the uniform of the new Royal Air Force.

The Duke and his new Duchess
are showered with rose petals
as they leave Buckingham Palace
for their honeymoon.

The Duke and Duchess, on honeymoon in 1923, pose for the photographers on the private golf course at Polesden Lacey in Surrey. This house, now the property of the National Trust, was lent to them by Mrs Ronnie Greville, a brewing heiress and society hostess. They continued their honeymoon at Glamis Castle.

Royal duties. With her husband looking on, the
Duchess tries an underhand throw at a coconut shy
at the Fresh Air Fund charity outing in July 1923.

The Duchess heads for the grouse butts through the heather with her brother-in-law, the Prince of Wales, whose cap and pipe are both at jaunty angles.

In early 1925 the Duke and Duchess tour East Africa, starting in Kenya before moving on to Uganda and then the Sudan. There is much shooting of big game and a visit to the Makwar dam on the Blue Nile, south of Khartoum in the Sudan, where they are seen here with colonial officials. The dam is used to irrigate new cotton plantations.

The Duchess engaged in typical royal duties: a tour of the industrial area of the Black Country in June 1925. In 1927 the Duke began a series of annual camps, mixing working-class boys with those from public schools.

The aerial railway at the British Empire Exhibition at Wembley in 1925. The Duke's stuttering delivery of a speech on this visit caused many to write him off as unfit for a royal role.

The Duke and
Duchess arrive by
train to go grouse
shooting at Glamis
on the 'Glorious
Twelfth' of August,
the start of the
season, in 1925.

(*Opposite*)
The future Queen
Elizabeth II, born
by Caesarean on
21 April 1926,
is admired by
her mother.
(*Right*) After the
presentation of
a new charter to
the Borough of
Ilford in Essex in
1926, the Duchess
is presented with
a teddy bear for
her daughter.

The Queen Mother has always been a keen supporter of the Girl Guides.
Here she inspects a troop at Glamis Castle before her marriage.

The Duke and Duchess of York at the Welsh National Eisteddfod held in Swansea in 1926.

In 1927 the Duke and Duchess embarked on the battleship HMS *Renown* for a six-month royal tour of Australia, New Zealand and Fiji. Here they are relaxing with a game of deck quoits.

The Duke, accompanied by the Duchess, opens
the new Federal Parliament Building in Canberra,
Australia, in May 1927. He makes an excellent
speech and then is confident enough to make a
second unscheduled one to the crowd of 20,000
gathered outside.

The Duchess is passionate about fishing, having been taught by her brothers in Scotland. She is seen here, during the 1927 tour, in pursuit of the giant rainbow trout for which Lake Taupo in New Zealand is famous.

More fishing in New Zealand, this time from a launch. It is a successful foray and the Duchess catches twenty fish in half an hour.

A day at the races, watching the Adelaide Cup during the Australian part of the 1927 tour.

The Duke and Duchess visit a traditional Maori house during their time in New Zealand in 1927.

The Duchess photographed in November 1927, some months after returning from the royal tour of Australia and New Zealand.

The Duke and
Duchess visit
Glasgow in 1928
for the launch
of the liner
Duchess of York.
The dockers in the
background go to
any length to get
a good view.

(*Above*) The Duchess jokes with some soldiers, disabled during the war, at their home in Putney in 1928. (*Opposite*) The St Patrick's Day Parade of the Irish Guards at Chelsea Barracks in 1928. The Duchess arrives for the annual presentation of bunches of shamrock to the regiment, a tradition begun by Queen Alexandra in 1901.

An informal
procession of the
royal generations
at a charity fête at
Balmoral in 1928:
Princess Elizabeth
in her pram, then
Queen Mary
followed by the
Duchess of York
with King George
V; Bertie brings
up the rear. Three
monarchs captured
in one picture.

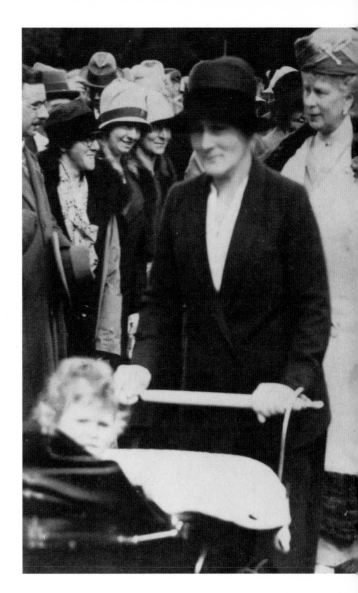

The Duchess seems amused rather than alarmed when a man
attempting to salute her and the Duke is restrained, August 1928.

The Duchess
was appointed
Colonel-in-Chief
of the King's Own
Yorkshire Light
Infantry in 1927.
Here she meets a
former Regimental
Sergeant-Major at
a parade in 1934,
shortly before
the regiment is
sent overseas.

Princess Margaret Rose is held in her mother's arms, in the year of her birth, 1930.

The Duchess, with her daughter Princess Elizabeth and niece Diana,
walks behind Princess Margaret's pram at a party at Glamis to celebrate
the Golden Wedding of her parents in 1931.

The Duchess of York driving to the ceremony of the
Trooping of the Colour by the Brigade of Guards in
June 1933, with Queen Mary and Princess Elizabeth.

The Royal Family
at the Epsom Derby
in 1934. Queen
Mary looks through
her binoculars at
something that the
Duchess of York has
spotted. The Duke
and Duchess of Kent
are on the left.

The Princesses Elizabeth (aged seven) and Margaret (aged three) try their
strength at an open air event in Scotland in 1933.

Led on by one of the corgis, which are to become such a feature of royal life in the years to come, the Duchess descends a railway bridge in 1935 with her two daughters.

Murrayfield rugby football stadium, Edinburgh 1935: the Duchess makes a point of talking to some crippled cubs at a rally of various children's organisations held to celebrate the Silver Jubilee of King George V.

A low bow for
the Duchess at a
garden party at
St James's Palace
for the National
Council for Child
Welfare, in 1935.

The Duchess sets off for her first flight, to the Brussels International
Exhibition, in 1935. The Duke learned to fly in 1919.

The Duchess releases pigeons as part of the celebrations to mark
King George V's Silver Jubilee in Edinburgh in 1935.

Princess Elizabeth stoops low so that she can see what lies ahead, as she leaves St Paul's Cathedral with her sister and parents, her uncle and her aunt – the Duke and Duchess of Kent – after the service for the Silver Jubilee of King George V in 1935.

The Duke sorts out his cine-camera aboard
one of the huge inter-war racing yachts –
note the size of the boom overhead – off
the Isle of Wight in 1935.

After opening a new building at the Girl's Heritage charity in 1936, the Duchess' eye is caught by a novel 'safety' cradle.

By unfurling a
flag, the Duchess
declares a new
block of flats open
in Somers Town, a
deprived area of
London, in 1936.

(*Opposite*) A dog lover through and through, the Duchess makes one of her Welsh corgis share this photograph taken in the garden of 145 Piccadilly, her and the Duke's London home, in 1936. (*Above*) In 1931 the people of Wales presented the two young Princesses with a miniature thatched cottage. It was erected in the grounds of the Yorks' weekend retreat, Royal Lodge, in Windsor Great Park. 'Us Four', as the Duke called his family, and their dogs pose in front of it in 1936.

King George V died late on 20 January, 1936. The Duchess, dressed in mourning, drives to Sandringham two days later to accompany the coffin to its lying-in-state in Westminster Hall.

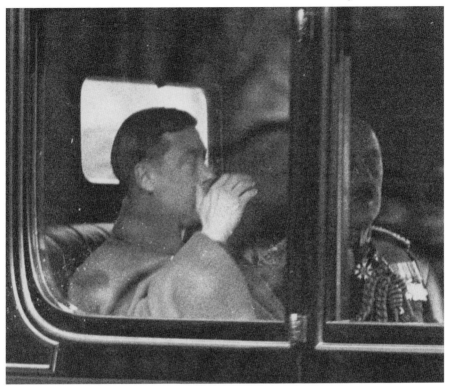

The new King, Edward VIII, drives to Buckingham Palace to hold the first formal levee of his reign in March 1936.

The Duchess in the sandpit of the playground just opened by her
on the site of the 18th-century Foundling Hospital, in Bloomsbury,
London, in 1936. The Hospital had moved to the country and its
fine buildings had been demolished.

The Duchess receives a bouquet in July 1936 when she opens the new playground on the Foundling Hospital site in Bloomsbury. Enough time has passed since George V's death for her to wear half-mourning.

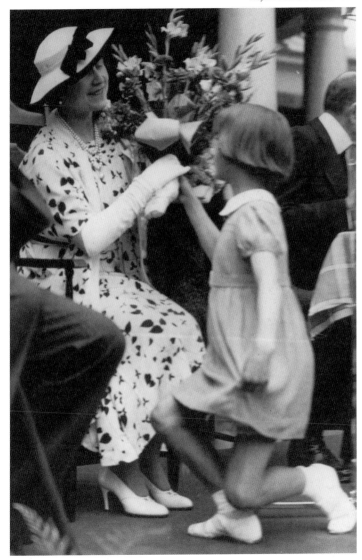

The Duchess takes her children to see the Bath Club in London in 1936.
It is here that they will be taught to swim.

The Yorks, with their beloved dogs, photographed in the summer of 1936 at Royal Lodge, Windsor.

Two brothers: King Edward VIII has just been received by the Duke of York in Aldershot where he has come to inspect battalions of the Coldstream and Scots Guards in 1936. The Duke is Colonel of the latter and both of the brothers wear its uniform.

The Duke and
Duchess about
to go down the
aptly named
Glamis Colliery in
County Durham
in July 1936. The
Duchess and her
ladies-in-waiting
are excused
having to wear
safety helmets.

(*Above*) Edward VIII with the new woman in his life, Mrs Wallis Simpson, an American divorcee, at the races. In August 1936 King Edward chartered a large yacht called the *Nahlin* for a cruise in the Adriatic. Wallis Simpson was among the party and (*opposite*) rests a proprietorial hand on the King as they go ashore from a motor launch.

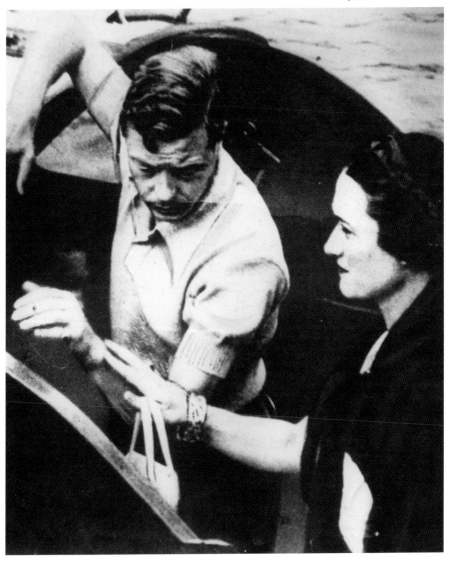

Long after the American and Continental press has broken the story, the British press at last ends its self-imposed silence to comment on the King and Mrs Simpson in December 1936. She went to France once the relationship was out in the open.

Edward VIII, now the ex-King, makes his abdication broadcast
from Windsor Castle on 11 December 1936. He was announced as
'His Royal Highness Prince Edward'.

The new King, George VI, returns to his home at 145 Piccadilly
after dining with his brother, who has just abdicated, at Royal Lodge
in Windsor Great Park on the evening of 11 December 1936.

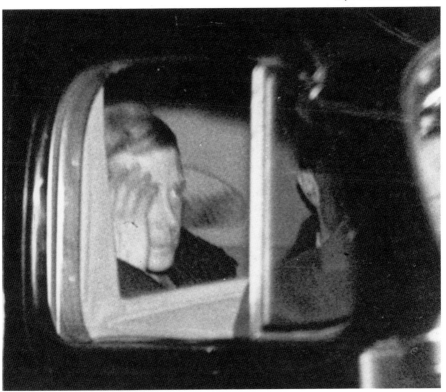

The Duke of Windsor, a title granted to him by his brother a few hours before, leaves Windsor Castle after making his abdication broadcast.

3. A Queen at War
1937–1945

After the 'Year of the Three Kings' from early 1936 to 1937, Albert, the reluctant King George VI, and his Queen have to repair the damage done to the image of the Crown in the wake of Edward VIII's abdication. So it seems no bad thing that she is the first Queen since Catherine Parr, sixth wife of Henry VIII, not to have been of royal birth. The Coronation in May 1937, heard by millions of British subjects on their wirelesses, is the perfect beginning to their reign. The following year they pay a state visit to France to give a boost to the *entente cordiale* as war with Hitler's Germany looms. The Queen, in mourning for her mother, impresses the French with a series of all-white ensembles, white being the alternative mourning colour to black. When the Prime Minister, Neville Chamberlain, returns on 30 September from meeting Hitler in Munich with what he claims is a guarantee of 'peace in our time', the King and Queen share the general relief and appear with him on the Buckingham Palace balcony. In 1939, Lord Tweedsmuir, the Governor-General of Canada, but better known as the writer John Buchan, is full of admiration for the Queen's 'perfect genius for the right kind of publicity' during the Royal Tour of North America, and she is to receive many such public acknowledgements. During the war an American newspaper calls the Queen the 'Minister for Morale' and her pronouncements show the determination which underlie her ceaseless activities. Asked about the possibility of the young Princesses being evacuated in 1940, she says: 'The children will not leave unless I do. I shall not leave unless their father does, and the King will not leave the country.'

Pomp and Circumstance: the Royal Family photographed in the Throne Room at Buckingham Palace shortly after returning from the Coronation ceremony in Westminster Abbey and still wearing their crowns, robes and trains, 12 May 1937.

It is 10.30 on the morning of
Coronation Day and the State Coach
leaves Buckingham Palace to go up the
Mall, passing by the monument to
Queen Victoria. It is pulled by eight
Windsor greys with four postilions,
six footmen, eight grooms and four
Yeomen of the Guard in attendance.

The most solemn moment of the Coronation ceremony as the Archbishop of Canterbury places the Crown of St Edward on the Monarch's head. The Queen, seated to the left, watches closely, as does every other person there. The present Queen and her sister are above and behind her.

The Queen herself has now been crowned and receives the Sceptre from the Archbishop, symbolic of the duties and responsibilities that she must share with her husband.

The Royal Family come out onto the balcony at
Buckingham Palace to allow their people another sight of
them in their crowns and Coronation robes. Behind are
some of the six maids of honour who carried the Queen's
eighteen-foot train of purple velvet. The two Princesses
have already learnt the peculiar energy-saving royal wave.

The King and Queen come out on the balcony at Buckingham Palace once
more on the evening of Coronation Day. The dramatic lighting from below
makes the most of the Queen's furs and tiara.

The Duke and
Duchess of
Windsor on their
wedding day,
3 June 1937, at
the Château de
Candé, near Tours.
It was lent to
them by a French-
born, naturalized
American, Charles
Debaux, who had
never met them
before they arrived
there. The day
before, the Duke
had heard from
his brother that
the Duchess was
not to be granted
the title 'Her
Royal Highness'.

The Royal Family in July
1937, at Holyrood House for
an inspection of the Royal
Company of Archers, the
King's Bodyguard in Scotland.
Queen Elizabeth talks to Lord
Elphinstone while Princess
Margaret is reduced to standing
on one leg by the magnificence
of the Archers' headgear.

The launch of the
Queen Elizabeth,
the world's largest
ocean liner, in
September 1938.
The Queen is
accompanied by
the two Princesses.

The *Queen Elizabeth* slides into the waters of the Clyde after the Queen has released a bottle of champagne to break on her bows. In fact, the ship starts to move prematurely and the Queen has to be quick when she pulls the lever. The *Queen Elizabeth* is to perform invaluable service during the war as a troopship, carrying thousands of GIs from the USA to fight in Europe and able to outpace any submarine with her turn of speed.

Sailing back from their Canadian tour in June 1939, the King and Queen are out on deck on *The Empress of Australia* with a cine-camera in case a spectacular iceberg is sighted.

In May and June 1939 the King and Queen went on a tour of Canada and a four-day visit to the United States. In Washington the heat is terrific, so the Queen makes use of her parasol (*opposite*) as she drives with President Roosevelt's wife Eleanor. Her charm sweeps America off its feet. (*Above*) The President and his wife with the Royal couple at his Hyde Park estate on the Hudson River above New York. His mother Sarah sits next to the Queen.

(*Left*)
The Queen leaves
a block of flats
in Wandsworth
in 1938, wearing
a dashing hat.
(*Opposite*)
The Royal Family
join in a song-
with-movement at
the King's camp
for boys near
Balmoral in 1939.

It's the day before war is declared in September 1939, and the Queen tours the ARP (Air Raid Protection) measures taken in Westminster.

In expectation of German bombers arriving over London as soon as war is declared, a massive evacuation of children has taken place. Here the Queen visits a school for evacuees from Battersea at Horsted Keynes in Sussex in November 1939. The boys are 'digging for victory', as the slogan goes, preparing ground for a crop of vegetables

(*Above*) The Queen talks to ARP workers after inspecting bomb damage in South-West London in 1940. (*Opposite*) All over Britain there are working parties of women like this one in Buckingham Palace in October 1939, where the Queen and members and wives of Household staff and the Royal Mews make clothes and surgical dressings for the Red Cross.

(*Opposite*)
The Queen talks
to a wounded RAF
pilot at a hospital
in Barnet in June
1940, just after the
evacuations from
Dunkirk. (*Right*)
The damage is
mounting: the
Queen speaks to
men demolishing
buildings rendered
unsafe by bombs.

On 13 September 1940 a
lone German bomber flies
up the Mall and drops its
load on Buckingham Palace.
The chapel and swimming
pool bear the brunt, and the
Queen remarks, 'I'm almost
glad we've been bombed.
Now I can look the East
End in the face.' Here she
inspects the ruins with the
King and Winston Churchill,
the Prime Minister.

(*Above*) The King and Queen visit the East End of London during the
Blitz in 1940. (*Opposite*) November 1940 and the Queen talks to London
children in an air raid shelter. It looks as though it is a Tube tunnel that
has been lined with wooden bunks.

Princesses Elizabeth and Margaret with
the Queen and a background of syringa
at Windsor in 1941.

The Queen, with
the King in the
background, talks
to some children
who have been
bombed out of
their homes. They
are having lunch
in a London rest
centre in
November 1940.

The Queen talks to a worker on a munitions factory production line who is assembling the fuses in the nose cones of shells.

The Queen and her two daughters in
identical outfits, taken in 1941 at Windsor.

The heavy air raids continue in 1941 and here the King and Queen talk to survivors against the background of a shattered terrace of houses.

An informal study of the King and Queen, taken in 1942, with the King getting logs for the fire and the Queen tuning the radio.

The Royal Family go to the Strand Theatre to see *Arsenic and Old Lace* in 1943. It is the Princesses' first evening visit to a West End theatre.

The National Gallery in Trafalgar Square, emptied of its picture collection for the duration of the war, becomes instead a concert hall for an immensely popular series of musical performances. People are ravenous for an hour or two of culture to help them escape the war. The Queen attends one and is seen sharing her neighbour's, Mrs EA Harris of Chadwell Heath, programme, since they are in short supply due to paper rationing.

The Royal Family conspicuously not wasting valuable petrol as they set out to inspect the harvest at Sandringham in 1943. The private golf course there now has a crop of oats and rye and, although the estate is highly mechanized by the standards of the day, there are still fourteen Land Girls working on it.

The Queen talks to a Land Girl who drives a tractor pulling a straw bailer during the 1943 harvest at Sandringham.

The King and Queen, accompanied by Princess Elizabeth, visit an RAF
bomber aerodrome at Witchford in Cambridgeshire in July 1944.
East Anglia and Lincolnshire are dotted with Bomber Command stations
from which the swarms of Lancasters and Halifaxes set out on most
nights for Germany. The pilots, navigators and gunners don't look a lot
older than the Princess.

Princess Elizabeth joined the ATS (Auxiliary Territorial Service) in 1944 and the following year she demonstrates her skills to her mother. When she joined, her mother reported, 'We had sparking plugs last night all the way through dinner.' After an inspection of her unit by the Princess Royal, the young Princess wrote, 'Spit and polish the whole day long. Now I realise what must happen when Papa and Mama go anywhere. That's something I shall never forget.'

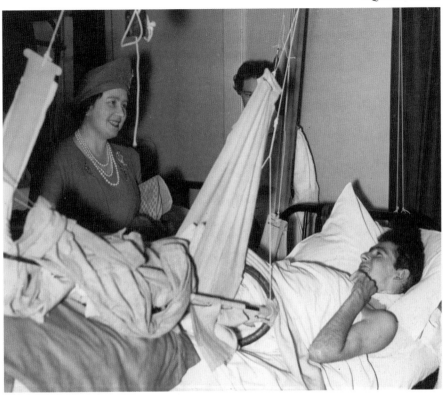

(*Opposite*) The King and Queen visit a US airbase in England in early 1944, as the numbers of American servicemen in the country reaches a peak before D-Day. (*Above*) A hospital visit to Botleys Park near Chertsey in October 1944.

The Royal Family flank Winston Churchill
on the balcony at Buckingham Palace on
VE day, 8 May 1945. Later the Princesses,
accompanied by Guards officers, mingled
with the crowd and sent back a message to
their parents: 'Come out, we want you to
see what it's like from this side.'

4. Grandmother and Widow

In 1946 the King and Queen become anxious when Princess Elizabeth falls in love with Prince Philip of Greece, fearing that she has simply succumbed to the first man to enter her life. A four-month tour of South Africa by the Royal Family the following year is meant to give her time to reflect, to give the King, exhausted by his wartime duties, a rest, and to strengthen General Smuts, the South African Premier, under attack from anti-British nationalist politicians. It fails in all three aims and so stressed is the Queen that when an African runs towards the royal car, she belabours him with her parasol, only to find that all he wants to do is give Princess Elizabeth a ten-shilling note as a twenty-first birthday present. To add to these problems, Princess Margaret is showing too much interest in a married man, the King's equerry, Group Captain Peter Townsend. Princess Elizabeth is married in November 1947, her wedding providing a counterweight to post-war austerity for the British people. The welcome news of royal births, Prince Charles in 1948 and Princess Anne in 1950, is only marred by the revelation that the King is seriously ill, and by 1951 it is apparent that he is in fact dying of lung cancer. On 16 February 1952 he is buried at Windsor, where the Lord Chamberlain breaks his white wand of office in two and throws the pieces onto the coffin in the vault below.

The Queen, a grandmother for the first time, holds the baby Prince Charles who has just been christened at Buckingham Palace on 15 December 1948. The month-old Charles is in the Royal Christening Robe of white silk and Honiton lace made for Queen Victoria's children. This is also the year of the King and Queen's silver wedding.

A real token of the return of peace: the young Princesses are taken by their parents to the reopening of the Royal Opera House, Covent Garden, in 1946. (During the war it served as a dance hall.) They see a performance of *Sleeping Beauty* by Sadler's Wells Ballet Company. Perhaps this is the moment when Princess Margaret falls in love with the artform that she is to give her patronage to in years to come.

The Royal Family have a moment of relaxation out of the public eye at Royal Lodge, Windsor, in 1946. As well as a corgi, there is Chin, another favourite, under the Queen's chair.

Another photograph taken on the same occasion as the previous one, and this time Chin has a lot more prominence.

(*Above*) Derby have won the cup at the first post-war Cup Final in 1946, and their captain, J Nichols, receives it from the King at Wembley Stadium. (*Opposite*) The first day of the first post-war Royal Ascot race meeting, and both mother and daughter show more than a passing interest in the runners and riders. The cup is waiting to be presented to the owner of the winner of one of that day's races.

A great gathering of Europe's royalty pose for a group photograph at the wedding of Princess Elizabeth to Prince Philip on 20 November 1947.

The King and Queen visit Salisbury, Southern Rhodesia (which today is Harare, Zimbabwe), during their four-month tour of Southern Africa. It is April 1947 and they are on their way to the State Opening of Parliament there.

The Royal Family arrive at Kroonstad station in South Africa
and transfer to a waiting car.

Having looked the East End in the face
following the bombing of their own home
in 1940, the King and Queen are able to
look each other in the eye in the comfort
of their apartments in 1948, the damage to
the Palace long since repaired.

The Queen at the reception at the
Victoria and Albert Museum for an
exhibition of Danish art in December
1948. As she talks to Princess Margaret,
Prince Philip leans forward to listen.
The King's sister, the Princess Royal, is
on the right and Princess Margareta of
Denmark second left.

The Queen unveils
a plaque on a
new block of flats
in Westminster
in July 1949,
part of the big
post-war building
programme to
replace slums and
bombed dwellings.

A surprise visit by the Queen to Mrs Cook's back garden in Bethnal Green, London, in July 1949. She is on a lightning tour of prize-winners in a competition sponsored by the London Garden Society.

It is Princess Anne's turn to be christened in October 1950, and the
Queen reaches out to catch Prince Charles who is bored by sitting
still for the photographs.

The Queen looks
in her handbag for
something with
which to distract
her grandson,
Prince Charles,
during his sister
Anne's christening.

In 1950 the Royal Norfolk Agricultural Show is held in the grounds of
Sandringham. Some children, determined to get a good look at the Queen,
have wriggled under the wall of the tent and are rewarded for their pains
by a word from her. Princess Margaret looks on.

The Queen plants a
cross with a poppy
on it at the Field
of Remembrance at
Westminster Abbey
in November 1950.
It is something
that she is to do
every year, right up
to the present day.

Royal Ascot is wet in 1950, so the Royal Family take refuge. The King smokes one of the cigarettes that have contributed to his health problems in recent years.

The King is too ill to take the salute at the Trooping of the
Colour in June 1951, so his eldest daughter deputizes for him
in Guards-style uniform. On the Buckingham Palace balcony
afterwards she draws the attention of Prince Charles to the RAF
fly-past overhead. She is flanked by Queen Mary and the Queen.

The King underwent major surgery in September 1951, so his brother the Duke of Gloucester deputizes for him at the Remembrance Day service at the Cenotaph in Whitehall that year. The Queen and other members of the Royal Family present a sombre spectacle.

The Queen talks to Gerald Barry, the Director of the Festival of Britain, on its opening day, 4 May 1951. Herbert Morrison, the Labour politician and moving spirit behind the Festival, is in spectacles on the left, with the Duke of Gloucester's two sons in front of him. Queen Mary sits in a wheelchair and the Dome of Discovery, built specially for the Festival on the South Bank, looms behind.

Prince Charles with his grandparents on his third birthday on
14 November 1951. The Queen holds Princess Anne. This is
the first photograph of the King since the operation to remove
his lung in September.

The King, Queen and Princess Margaret admire a rose grower's display at the annual Chelsea Flower Show, which was held in the grounds of the Royal Hospital in 1951.

(*Above*) Princess Elizabeth and her husband, the Duke of Edinburgh, are setting off on a Commonwealth tour on 31 January 1952, and the Queen, Princess Margaret and the King leave the aircraft after saying goodbye. This is the last time the Princess sees her father. A little later (*opposite*), the King and Queen watch the plane depart for Nairobi in Kenya while the Prime Minister, Winston Churchill, looks through the glass doors below.

(*Above*) Londoners gather to read of the death of King George VI at Sandringham on 6 February 1952 in that day's evening papers. (*Opposite*) On the Saturday following the King's death the crowd at Craven Cottage, Fulham Football Club's ground, observes a minute's silence before the game against Newcastle begins. Players all over Britain wear black arm bands and at a number of grounds a band plays *Abide With Me*.

Three Queens
mourn a father,
son and husband.

(*Left*) The Queen Mother is driven from Buckingham Palace to Westminster Hall where she will await the arrival of the cortège accompanying her husband's body, 11 February 1952. (*Opposite*) The King's coffin has arrived from Sandringham by train, at King's Cross station. Guardsmen carry it to the waiting gun carriage that will take it to Westminster Hall for the lying-in-state, 11 February 1952. The Queen, Princess Margaret, Prince Philip and the Duke and Duchess of Gloucester watch.

5. Queen Mother

1953–1979

In May 1953 the Queen Mother, already affectionately shortened to 'Queen Mum' by most of the British population, moves a short distance down the Mall from the Palace to Clarence House, which becomes her London home. She continues to use Royal Lodge at Windsor Great Park and Birkhall on the Balmoral estate, but in 1954 she buys the remote, windswept and semi-derelict Castle of Mey on the Caithness coast in north-east Scotland. Once restored, it is something of an extravagance, as she only uses it for six weeks each year. The 1950s and 1960s are characterised by a busy work schedule and several ups and downs on the domestic front. In 1955, after much agonising, Princess Margaret decides she cannot marry the divorced Peter Townsend: the Prime Minister, Anthony Eden, has made it clear that, if she does, she would have to live abroad, initially at least. She finally weds Antony Armstrong Jones in 1960. In 1956, the Queen Mother becomes the first member of the Royal Family to start using a helicopter regularly. She is later to say, 'The chopper has changed my life as conclusively as that of Anne Boleyn.' In the same year her horse Devon Loch, ridden by Dick Francis, suddenly and memorably does the splits when in the lead and in sight of the finishing post in the Grand National steeplechase. The development of modern aircraft encourages the Queen Mother to become the first British royal to fly round the world on her 1958 tour, a distinct aid in her busy round of duties at home and abroad. The Queen Mother is Colonel-in-Chief of thirteen regiments and corps, Honorary Colonel of four others, and Commander-in-Chief of the WRNS, WRAC and WRAF, which explains in part why there are so many calls on her time.

A radiant Queen Mother bids farewell to her hosts in Salisbury, Southern Rhodesia (now Harare, Zimbabwe), at the end of her 1957 African tour, and knocks spots off Hollywood as she does so.

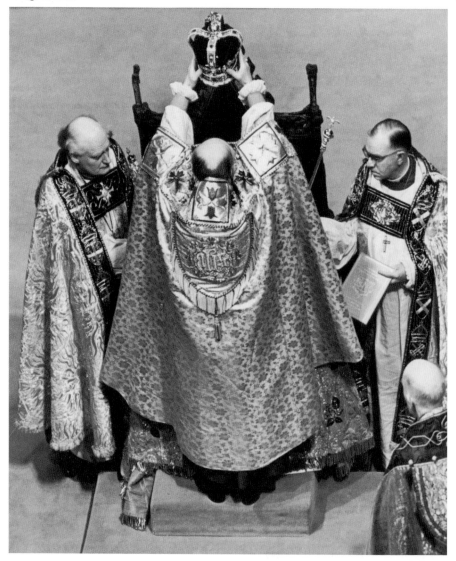

(*Opposite*) A slightly surreal photograph of the culmination of Queen Elizabeth II's Coronation, on 2 June 1953, as the Archbishop of Canterbury is about to place the crown on her head. The Queen has disappeared behind his enveloping cope and the only clue to her presence is the Sceptre that she holds, which sticks out at an angle. (*Above*) A royal group in the Throne Room at Buckingham Palace after the Coronation, with Prince Charles and Princess Anne standing on a small island between the trains of their mother and grandmother.

(*Above*) A second generation makes use of the Little Welsh House at Windsor: Prince Charles and his grandmother in 1954. (*Opposite*) A photograph taken at the same time as the previous one, at Royal Lodge, but now Princess Anne joins her brother. There are no leaves on the trees, so this must be winter sunshine.

(*Above*) Princess Anne greets the Queen Mother in November 1954 as she returns from a triumphant visit to the United States and Canada. 'Who is going to be interested in the middle-aged widow of a king?' she said before she went. How wrong she was. (*Opposite*) Princess Margaret and the Queen Mother wave to Prince Charles and Princess Anne in April 1954 as they set sail from Portsmouth in the Royal Yacht *Britannia* to meet up with their parents, who are on their way home from a Commonwealth Tour, in the Mediterranean.

The Queen Mother watches anxiously as the Queen's horse, Countryman III, falters at a jump on the cross-country course at the Badminton Horse Trials in 1956. The Queen, on the other hand, is intent on capturing the moment on film.

The Queen Mother greets the jockey Dick Francis, who is to ride one of her horses, in the paddock before a race. The Queen Mother bought her first steeplechaser, Monaveen, for £1,000, with the Queen in 1949. In the 1960s she had as many as nineteen horses in training.

African children gather to greet the Queen Mother in Northern Rhodesia (now Zambia) in July 1957. They are at the Roan Antelope copper mine, down which she went to a depth of 1,400 feet.

Twins Laura and
Lillian present the
Queen Mother with
a bouquet when she
visits the African
Induction School in
the Copper Belt in
Northern Rhodesia
(Zimbabwe).

In January 1958 the Queen Mother starts
a gruelling world tour, during which she
visits Canada, Honolulu, Fiji, New Zealand,
Australia and Tasmania. Here she is in
Australia, about to set off in a motor launch
with a mass of yachts waiting to escort her.

The Queen Mother listens to a speech at the Guildhall in the City of London at a reception to welcome her home in March 1958, after her world tour.

An entirely natural combination: the Queen Mother and a Scottish pipe band in June 1958.

(*Above*) The Queen Mother, who got to know him well when he led the
Free French in London during the war, lunches with General de Gaulle, now
President of France, at the Elysée Palace in Paris in April 1959. (*Opposite*)
The Queen Mother in her element, reeling at the Caledonian Ball in London,
May 1959. Her Lord Chamberlain, the Earl of Airlie and father of Angus
Ogilvy, the husband of her niece Princess Alexandra, is on her right.

(*Opposite*) Mother and daughter indulge in their favourite pastime, going to the races. Here they are at Epsom in June 1959 for the Oaks, won that year by Petite Etoile (a good sobriquet for the Queen Mother). (*Right*) At the races again, this time Royal Ascot in 1960.

The Queen Mother follows at a more sedate pace behind an exuberant Princess Anne (clutching a confetti basket) at the wedding of her second daughter. Additional members of her family include Prince Charles (left, wearing a kilt) and, next to him and half turning, Sir David Bowes-Lyon, the Queen Mother's brother.

Princess Margaret walks down the nave of Westminster Abbey on the arm of her husband, the Earl of Snowdon, Antony Armstrong-Jones, after their marriage in May 1960.

Princess Margaret, with the Duke of Edinburgh, who is to give her away, on the way to her wedding.

Celebrating her sixtieth birthday at Clarence House in 1960,
the Queen Mother sits with Prince Andrew (the Duke of York)
on her knee while Princess Anne introduces him to botany.

The Fab Four, the Beatles, meet the Queen Mother in the line-up of performers at the Royal Variety Show in November 1963, the year in which they shot to fame.

(*Opposite*) The Queen Mother at the annual Garter Ceremony held at St George's Chapel, Windsor Castle, in June 1962. The robes and headgear worn by members of the Order of the Garter can be deeply unflattering, but not when worn by her. (*Above*) In November 1964 three of the Queen Mother's horses are winners in one afternoon's racing at Folkestone. Here she is with the first one, Arch Point.

In 1966 the Queen Mother returns to Australia where she visits the seventeen-year-old Prince Charles at Timbertop School, which is in the bush, north of Melbourne, before going on to New Zealand. She talks here with Maori girls after they have performed their 'poi' dance in the sportsdome at Rotorua.

Nearly all the Queen Mother's free time in New Zealand is given over to fishing, although she does not have much luck. When she finally catches a trout, she notes that 'It would have been better to get one out of the deep freeze.' A glimpse of the famous pearls can be caught beneath the waterproofs.

The Duke of Windsor, accompanied by his
wife, attends his first public ceremony with
the Queen since his abdication, when she
unveils a plaque in memory of Queen Mary,
his mother, at her former home, Marlborough
House in the Mall. The date, 7 June 1967,
is the centenary of the birth of Queen Mary.
The Duchess of Windsor looks on as the
Queen Mother is kissed by the Duke.

Another Royal Variety Performance, in 1968, and this time it is
The Supremes who get to meet the Queen Mother.

The Investiture of Prince Charles as the Prince of Wales at Caernavon Castle in Wales in 1969. The Queen Mother looks on with Princess Margaret and Lord Snowdon who is responsible for some of the design at the Investiture, including the tunic he himself is wearing, which has the Prince of Wales' feathers on the collar, and the chairs behind.

Grandchildren gather to wish the Queen
Mother a happy seventieth birthday in
August 1970: Prince Edward (left), Lady
Sarah Armstrong-Jones and her brother
Viscount Linley. Her hat is more than a
match for the geraniums.

The Queen Mother talks to the Prince of Wales at the 1972 Garter Procession. They are preceded by the Duke of Norfolk and Earl Mountbatten; Field Marshal Viscount Montgomery leads.

The Royal Variety Show in 1972: Impresario Bernard Delfont ushers the
Royal Party to their seats, with a sea of carnations in the foreground.

The Royal Family and European royalty cluster round Princess Anne and Captain Mark Phillips after their wedding in 1973 for the traditional group photograph.

The Royal Family have often been spectators at the Badminton Horse Trials, a three-day event held each year in Gloucestershire at the home of the Duke of Beaufort. It has been a chance for the public to see them at their most informal, as in these pictures taken in the 1970s.

On a splendidly sunny afternoon in 1975 the Queen Mother arrives for another day's racing at Royal Ascot.

(*Above*) The Queen Mother in a magnificent sequinned dress, with a red lacquer cabinet on a silver stand in the background – a study by the famous fashion photographer Norman Parkinson from 1975. (*Right*) Another Norman Parkinson picture, but this time a close-up that allows the Queen Mother's stunning jewellery to be clearly seen.

6. Great Grandmother

The Queen Mother's first great-grandchild, Princess Anne's son Peter Phillips, is born in 1977, the year of the Queen Elizabeth II's Silver Jubilee. In 1979 the Queen Mother becomes Lord Warden of the Cinque Ports and Constable of Dover Castle. The Ports are Sandwich, Dover, Romney, Hythe and Hastings, and, while she has the right to certain 'fishes royal', she is also responsible for burying stranded whales. On her eightieth birthday there are special garden parties, a Covent Garden gala, and a service of thanksgiving at St Paul's Cathedral. In 1982 she has to go into hospital in order to have a fishbone removed, saying, 'After all these years of fishing, the fish are having their revenge.' Prince Andrew is serving in the Falklands War as a helicopter pilot and Prince William is born to Princess Diana and Prince Charles. In 1986 she attends the burial of the Duchess of Windsor at Windsor. In 1989 the Queen Mother returns to Canada fifty years after her first visit. In 1991 she still carries out over one hundred official engagements. In 1992 and 1998 she has hip replacement operations to replace. In between she plays a central part in the celebrations for the fiftieth anniversary of VE Day, in 1995. Only now is she letting up on official engagements, but even a few weeks before her hundredth birthday it is reported that she outstays many, until well after one in the morning, at the great Birthday Ball at Windsor Castle, and she makes a speech of thanks at a lunch in her honour at the Guildhall.

The Queen Mother holds William, the son of Prince Charles and Princess Diana, after his christening on 4 August 1982, her birthday.

Six grandchildren join their grandmother on her eightieth birthday
at Buckingham Palace: Princes Edward, Charles and Andrew; Viscount
Linley; Princess Anne and Lady Sarah Armstrong-Jones.

Norman Parkinson
photographs the
Queen Mother
again, this time to
commemorate her
eightieth birthday.

One of the most popular of royal
photographs: Norman Parkinson uses
his skills as a fashion photographer to
produce this triple portrait of mother and
daughters, which was also taken on the
Queen Mother's eightieth birthday.

A month before their own marriage, Prince Charles and Lady Diana Spencer, together with the Queen Mother and Princess Margaret, attend the wedding of Nicholas Soames, a grandson of Winston Churchill, June 1981.

Wearing a wonderful powder-puff hat, the Queen Mother, accompanied by Prince Andrew, returns from Prince Charles' wedding in July 1981. There is altogether a remarkable collection of headgear here, what with the RAF band in the foreground and the coachman and two footmen behind.

Princess Diana's family are on the right and the Royal Family on the left in this group photograph taken after her wedding to Prince Charles.

King Harald of Norway, Princess Diana, Princess Alice, Duchess of
Gloucester, and the Queen Mother at the Cenotaph service on
Remembrance Sunday, 1981.

The Queen Mother talks to Chelsea Pensioners on Founder's Day at the Royal Hospital in 1981. The Pensioners wear springs of oak leaves in memory of King Charles II, the Founder, who hid from the Roundheads in an oak tree after the Battle of Worcester in 1651.

The Queen Mother, with a posy of white heather, at the Braemar
Gathering in 1982. Princess Diana wears a version of a glengarry cap and
Prince Charles a kilt of Balmoral tartan.

On a visit to Paris in 1982, the Queen Mother is received by
President and Madame Mitterand.

The Queen Mother in 1984 with the famous transparent umbrella that she uses so that she remains visible in the rain. The expressions on the faces of the crowd say it all.

Another speciality of the Queen Mother is her veiled hats, and here is a splendid one that she wears to open a hospice at West Ham, London.

Has the Queen Mother backed a near-winner at the Derby in 1985?
No need to ask the same of the Queen.

Princess Diana and the Queen Mother are applauded as they arrive at Ascot in 1986.

Some very young dancers file past the Royal party at the Braemar
Gathering in 1986. Their kilts combine with the outfits of the Duchess
of York, Princess Diana, the Queen Mother and the Queen to produce
what can only be called a riot of colours.

A gathering outside Clarence House for the Queen Mother's eighty-sixth
birthday: the Yorks, the Waleses and her two daughters.

The Queen Mother presents shamrock to
the Irish Guards on St Patrick's Day, 1987,
as she does each year. Whatever she is
saying said has extracted a smile out of the
NCO and officer on her left.

The Queen and the Queen Mother on the balcony at Buckingham Palace during the commemoration of the fiftieth anniversary of VE Day, 8 May 1995.

The Queen Mother presents a cup at the 1981 Royal Smithfield Show.
She had a prize-winning herd of cattle on her estate at the Castle of Mey
in Caithness for many years.

The Queen
Mother talks to
the owners of two
prize-winning
sheep at the same
show. One of the
after-dinner songs
that the Queen
Mother is known
to have performed
is Sir Walter Scott's
'Ca' the yowes
to the knowe'
('Call the ewes to
the hillock').

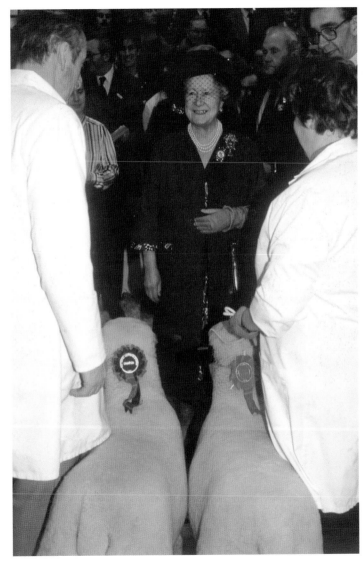

The Queen
Mother arrives
for lunch at the
Guildhall in the
City of London
in 1997.

Wiping away a tear? The Queen Mother has just placed her small wooden cross in the Field of Remembrance at Westminster Abbey for the dead of two world wars, November 1997.

Outside the church at Sandringham Church on Christmas Day 1998 with Eugenie and Beatrice, daughters of the Duke and Duchess of York and great-granddaughters of the Queen Mother.

Sophie Rhys Jones, soon to be the wife of Prince Edward, goes to the Trooping of the Colour with her future husband and the Queen Mother in 1999.

In her hundredth year the Queen Mother is still there to present the Irish Guards with their annual shamrock.

The Queen Mother leaves St Paul's Cathedral after the service to celebrate her one hundredth birthday on 11 July 2000. Naturally Queen Elizabeth II was there, as were four generations of the Royal Family and a crowd of thousands. Leading the service, Dr George Carey, the Archbishop of Canterbury said the Queen Mother had entered into the hearts of the British people, and, he told her, 'your own heart has been open to them ever since.'

Index

About the pictures in this book

This book was created by The Hulton Getty Picture Collection which comprises over 300 separate collections and 18 million images. It is a part of Getty Images Inc., with over 70 million images and 30,000 hours of film.

How to buy or license a picture from this book

All non-Hulton images are credited individually below.

Picture licensing information	Online access	Buying a print
For information about licensing any image in this book, please phone + 44 (0)20 7579 5731, fax: +44 (0)20 7266 3154 or e-mail chris.barwick@getty-images.com	For information about Getty Images and for access to individual collections go to www.hultongetty.com. Go to www.gettyone.com for creative and conceptually oriented imagery and www.gettysource.com for editorial images.	For details on how to purchase exhibition quality prints call The Hulton Getty Picture Gallery, phone + 44 (0)20 7276 4525 or e-mail hulton.gallery@getty-images.com

Picture Credits